Blow On A Trumpet Drunk Until You Throw Up

Your Breakfast

I0436454

By Darryl Harrison

Copyright 2012, 2015 Darryl Harrison

Bird Poop Edition, License Notes

Table Of Contents

A Wild Sunday

Mr. Dayha Lamont would be a fierce-looking black dude. He sat in Elfar's tavern, sipping his seventh Corona. He appeared to be miserable. He had been pulled over for a broken taillight, a youthful girl had kissing him. The cops smelled marijuana and beer on his breath. They checked the vehicle and discovered a bag of weed. Once the dude got out of jail, he was initially terminated from his busboy job.

He had been hanging around in the tavern for his buddy Melvin Hernandez. He spoke with Elfar regarding a job right here. Elfar appeared to be a moron, not because he had been half-black and

Spanish, due to the fact, he was on that dope and the man kept getting people's cocktails mixed-up. The slime-breath appreciated crack cocaine and also Amanita Muscaria. He'd this real funny donkey on stage telling very cool jokes and passing gas all the time. He'd a massive container of Cobra beer on stage. So when he got thirst he'd guzzle. Everyone enjoyed themselves. Mr. Lamont believed the donkey was very funny and was getting drunk. The donkey kept burping and passing gas. The last part of the act was the donkey smoking dope and he began reciting Shakespeare beautifully.

Mr. Lamont loathed coming over to this tavern, but he didn't have sufficient funds to go somewhere else. He got upset whenever he walked into the restroom to doo-doo, due to the fact there wasn't any door on the stalls and bums would come in and beg. For this reason on one occasion, he soon began tossing doo-doo at them until they ran out of the place.

What he did enjoy in regards to the tavern they constantly played out the greatest Jazz music. Despite the fact that the majority of the performers were fourth-rate, it didn't make a difference.

"Well, I want a job, Elfar," Mr. Lamont stated sharply with a smirk.

"Times are actually difficult, baby. Possibly later on in the month, dog," Elfar explained strongly.

"What the heck have you been undertaking back there?" Lamont asked sharply.

"Dog, I'm jacking-off! Dog, I usually develop the greatest orgasms seeing these kinds of fantastic acts on stage," Elfar said strongly with a laugh.

"Stop! Don't do this here, dude! It's not cool, bruh," Lamont said bitterly.

"I'm nearly done, dog. Don't ruin a great orgasm. You feel me?" Elfar said bitterly.

"Oh Lord. You have your cat doing that, too," Mr. Lamont snapped.

"Hell, yes. This cats recently has been doing it a great deal these days," Elfar said happily.

"Please make him quit. Dude, I can't endure this stuff. Or even this awful tavern. This spot smells just like a hundred thousand animals farted in this place. I can't even smell the great cannabis. Even so the unclothed barmaids are good, apart from the red head; she has got to scrub her booty little better," Mr. Lamont said hotly.

He chucked a beer bottle at the feline.

"Bruh, are you crazy?" Elfar said hotly.

"Shut up, frog-breath!" Mr. Lamont said sharply.

The barmaids had been strolling about smoking weed as well as making love with all the creeps that arrived up in this joint. Previous Lamont experienced lovemaking with this blond broad on the bar stool.

"Shut up, bum! All you do is whine," Elfar said bluntly, guzzling a bottle of Cobra.

"Give me a hit on that joint, with your other hand, homeboy," Mr. Lamont stated snugly.

Mr. Lamont spoke with Melvin on the phone. Melvin had been a guy he busted tables with at a coffee house.

"Hey, dog? Where have you been, bro-bro?" Mr. Lamont asked strongly.

"Bruh, I'm with my son. We're at Brook Bears Hospital. The little-homeboy ate a canary," Melvin explained sharply with a laugh. "The doctor's shirt is wide open and she would like to make love to me after the surgical treatment," he said cheerfully.

"I got you, baby," Mr. Lamont said happily.

"Are you stoned, gee?" Melvin snapped.

"Always," Lamont said sharply with laugh.

"What about Sunday?" Melvin said strongly.

"Dude, that's still on, at my crib," Lamont said strongly.

"Bruh. The Lakers' are likely to cream the New York Nicks. Dude, I'll deliver the alcohol. Dude, you'll be able to provide the marijuana," Mr. Hernandez said happily.

"For sure," Mr. Lamont said cheerfully. "And maybe some fly girls."

"For sure, dog," Melvin said clearly.

"I hope the little G's all right," Mr. Lamont said firmly.

"That homeboy will be okay with his hard head," Melvin said firmly and hung up.

Mr. Lamont was ready to depart when a nice-looking black chick got on stage. The woman had four big breast. Plus she brought the Afro back in fashion. She seemed to be lengthy and scrumptious. She contributed this pooch and cat with her, a Pointer, positioning him on a stool. She had this long stick. She swung that thing about like a conductor, the dog sang opera and rock 'n roll, and her four-year-old son performed the drums as well as the cat rapped and played the piano. It was the coolest. It had been the coolest show he experienced. The audience adored it.

"Don't start beaten-off again," Mr. Lamont stated sharply.

"I'm not, brother," Elfar stated firmly.

"Your cat has slimy green sperm?" Mr. Lamont said strongly.

"Yes, isn't that awesome?" Elfar said happily.

"Yeah, if you're six, bruh," Mr. Lamont said hotly.

"Want another Cobra, baby?" Elfar said strongly with a smirk.

"Is it on the house?" Lamont snapped.

"Slime you. This economy sucks and I can't afford to," Elfar said firmly.

"Dog, I demand a job. Barf on the economy, homeboy. Old blood, I'll clean your rotten toilets full of doo-doo stains with my tongue. I'll suck that furry beast's penis," Mr. Lamont stated sharply.

"No! I don't hire drunks. Besides my cat doesn't permit broke bums blowing him," Elfar said strongly.

"Slime you punk!" Mr. Lamont said hotly.

"Then jet homey!" Elfar said hotly.

"She's the best act you've ever got," Mr. Lamont said strongly, glancing at the audience, it's was larger now.

"I'm likely to make love to her right after the show," Mr. Elfar claimed strongly.

"Why not a threesome?" Lamont snapped.

"For Sure, bruh," Elfar said strongly.

Right after the show, all of them had some beer. Lamont put some Cobra inside a bowl for the dog and cat to share. All of them had outrageous sex with strawberry jam along with the dog and cat.

The crowds of folks were a tad too much for Lamont. Yet he had been happy, simply because he never observed a dog sing before. The dog possessed a better voice than the majority of folks he heard. The cat rapped and played the piano great. He got on his Harley and road that mother down the sidewalk at 80 mph, running over folks, knocking over street-vender's stuff and rode throughout the Eldorado casino, causing a lot of destruction.

The next day he went in search of employment. He put in an application at each and every casino. He traveled to every supermarket. A weird dude with an inflectionless speech resided in a barn. He desired Lamont to clean up all the horse and human doo-doo for thirty bucks. Yet he'd phone him if he required him. He traveled to Saturday & Sunday warehouse, jobs for the weekend exclusively. In Reno, warehouse work opportunities happen to be difficult to come across, given that they compensated a great deal. He threw up some blue pink stuff on the door.

While Mr. Lamont had been at his shabby room smoking an enormous marijuana stick as he masturbated, his mother barged in, and her face etched in desperation. Blood ran out of her nose just like a fire hydrant.

"Help me, child," she cried sharply.

"The blood...oh darn! Momma, what did you do? Have you been drinking again?" Mr. Lamont said franticly.

"No, never, boy!" she said snugly.

Blood had been all over the place just like a horror movie-set. He settled her down and retrieved a damp cloth.

"You're smoking that stuff again, boy?" she complaincd loudly.

"Not now, momma," he stated sharply, pressing the cloth on her nose, moving her head back gently.

"Momma, you're gonna be okay. So why didn't you call a doctor?"

"I hate doctors, boy," she snapped.

Once everything seemed to be cool, Lamont took his mother to the medical center for observation. He remained with her until they discharge her. It wasn't serious. Her blood pressure was high. And she had to quit salt, or minimize it.

Mr. Lamont was back in his room drinking Canadian Mist. The neurotic landlady had just left lugging a blowtorch. She threatened to put his butt on fire if he didn't come up with some dough real quickly. He offered her some marijuana and made love to her in the hallway. Therefore, she chose to give him some more time. Then he received great news that Saturday & Sunday warehouse wished for him to come in for a job interview.

On Saturday morning, he met with a sweet-candy black dude, who'd be his boss. Mr. Lamont dressed in a filthy blue suit, terribly old, torn badly and wrinkly, because he couldn't afford to get it cleaned or buy a new one. He smelled like marijuana, beer and doo-doo. His hair required brushing and washing. He required shaving.

"I'm so delighted you arrived. I'd been pleased with your application," he stated cheerfully.

"Why?" Mr. Lamont snapped.

"I don't know. You've got paid to assist old ladies jump on a bar stools. Your previous occupation must have been exciting. Dog, I believe all of us ought to assist the elderly," he said strongly with a laugh.

"Nah. homey, I pushed old broads off of bar stools," Mr. Lamont said sharply with a laugh.

"Great," he stated happily.

"It was," Lamont said happily.

The supervisor giggled. "My name is Bruce Wajer. I'll be supervising your work; bruh. Miss Carol Gurry may be assisting you," Mr. Wajer said cheerfully.

"The blond with the horse-butt, bruh?" Mr. Lamont asked strongly, holding on to his dick.

"Yeh, her," Wajer said cheerfully.

Wajer's breath smelled slimy. His entire body smelled as though he spent the morning swimming in Brut cologne.

"You smell of marijuana and liquor. Are you high, dog?" Mr. Wajer asked seriously.

"You better believe it, baby," Mr. Lamont said strongly with a laugh.

"Oh, child. We can't have folks working right here on drugs," Wajer said bitterly.

"Well, folks on drugs need to eat and pay their mortgages as well," Mr. Lamont said firmly.

"I'll let it slide this time around, but no more. It impairs your capability to carry out at your best," Wajer said cheerfully.

Wajer sent Mr. Lamont off to deal with the lions. Mr. Wajer shook his butt much better than nearly all the women he'd seen did.

Miss Curry had him folding corny shirts and stuff, setting them in boxes, which had been fairly simple. He marked a number of them using a black marker. She'd monster boobs, yet breath just like hot-dogs, with hefty on the onions. The kinda girls he's usually stuck with. Her body odor wasn't too cool either. She offered him slinky body language. She kept touching his private area and butt all the time. A very horny white girl.

Once the boxes had been full, a large blond dude on a forklift hauled everything away. He never put on a shirt.

"Not bad for your first day," she mentioned cheerfully.

"Thank you, baby," he stated strongly with a laugh and spit on the table.

"Why have you been averting me?" she said strongly.

"Well I consider work major, boo," he said firmly.

"Are ya gay, honey?" she asked slyly.

"No. Not that it's negative," Mr. Lamont said strongly.

"If you're there's Robert. Dude, I hear he provide a mean blowjob," she said happily.

"Bruh, I'll take your word for it," Lamont said sharply.

"You get high, bruh?" she asked strongly.

"Who doesn't?" he snapped.

"You have got to be mindful in Nevada. They're difficult," she said firmly.

"So what? Blood, I get high regularly. Baby, it's just like pissing with me," Mr. Lamont said strongly.

"Baby, be careful," she said.

"Ah, leave me alone, woman!" Lamont stated bitterly.

The employees had been mainly women and gays. Everyone appeared to be cool with Mr. Lamont. Everybody acquired humorous moments about working here.

At lunch, Mr. Lamont could stash a variety of shirts outdoors at the rear of the building to take home. He spent his break drinking at the casino bar across the street. He kept poking sexy cocktail waitresses in the butt crack with his finger every time they strolled past. He also enjoyed basketball, football and hockey on the big screen.

Once he came back to work, he threw-up on one of the table. It was an accident. He folded shirts until his arms fell off and listened to worthless bull, and couldn't wait until stopping time. Don't get him wrong he had been thrilled to have employment. Yet this job wasn't challenging enough. He required something much more than an easy job.

Once he got home, he smoked marijuana and drank Olde English by the gallons. He gazed at some wrestling, WWF. He couldn't understand why a variety of barrel-shaped dudes and broads tossed each other about just like ragdolls'. But once the drugs took it's effect everything seemed in its appropriate place, even the freakiest stuff. He thought he noticed one of the chicks slamming a bear about in the ring. At some point, he saw the bear having sex with one of the black chicks and the crowd went nuts. The audience seemed to be large. Yet folks appeared as if lizards. And huge cabbages flied across the ring with big red wings. A huge hawk swooped down on the wrestler raised him out of the ring, dropping him into the audience.

Then this crowd went nuts and rushed the ring, removing all his and her clothes and folks had outrageous sex. Exactly what did Pascual place in his marijuana?

About Sunday morning, Mr. Lamont came back to work. He'd stood outdoors drinking Cobra beer until folks turned up, Wajer unlocked the door, and folks poured in. His boss's breath still smelled poopy. He must have been licking someone's butt. Miss Gurry turned up sporting a tight peach-colored dress. She smelled just like sweaty hogs nuts. She'd one purple eye and one blue. Her blond hair was now bouncy. She greeted Mr. Lamont by squeezing his private area. She was an unusual broad.

Once the good-looking fork-lifter didn't show- Wajer had Mr. Lamont work the monster. The Sunday had been catastrophic. Mr. Lamont was stoned and he kept crashing the forklift into shelves and knocking over big boxes and clothes fell out everywhere. He ran over workers and rammed the beast into walls and through the office, destroying everything. Three gay men got into a fight over a man. A number of adolescent punks started a fire in the back when they dropped a joint in a box packed with paper and shirts. Mr. Lamont drove the forklift through the big shop window and even throughout the parking lot, crashing into vehicles, ramming into a bus stop bench where a young black girl and an old woman sat. Lastly, he left the huge bitch in the middle of the street.

During lunch, Mr. Lamont stole several boxes of shirts through all the commotion, stashing them in the bushes. He captured a Broadway show in the casino across the street. He drank Budweiser and ate a sub sandwich. When he came back to the warehouse, the police had been there. Thus, he went home.

Mr. Lamont spent the evening at his rat-infested room, smoking marijuana and drinking Colt 45. A number of the workers were preparing to file a personal injury suit against him. Yet he was too stoned to care. He was ready for Melvin to phone any minute. But there was a knock on the door. But he told that bastard to phone first. He opened the door and Carol Gurry came in.

"Dude, I'm sorry to burst in on you. Dude, I'd to see you again," she stated excitedly.

"So you dig chocolate?" Mr. Lamont said strongly.

"Sure," she said cheerfully.

"You desire a joint, girl?" Mr. Lamont said strongly. "Because only stoners can get down with me."

"Yeah, sure," she stated sharply with a smile, strolling past Mr. Lamont and sat on a ratty old sofa.

"Baby, I got Jamaica shit (Ganga). It's truly fly," he explained strongly with a smile, passing a massive marijuana stick to her.

He lit her joint. Miss Gurry took a good drag.

"Do you like to make love?" she asked happily.

"Who doesn't?" Lamont snapped.

"Do you prefer black widows?" she asked cheerfully.

"When those things ain't in my damn bed," Mr. Lamont said firmly with a laugh.

Mr. Lamont got a forty-ounce bottle of Colt .45 and opened it. He had taken a long suck on it. Then he passed it to Miss Gurry. She guzzled the bottle. He took a drag from the joint.

"The reason I came up here is because I needed to make love to you. Since I met you at work I've desired you," she said sharply, eyeing him fondly.

"Baby, I could tell," Lamont said strongly, guzzling beer.

"Do you want to make love?" she asked sharply.

"Yeah, but my buddy is coming over. We intended to see the game," Lamont said strongly. "Maybe we can have a threesome. You feel me?"

"Dude...I only got eyes for you. I'm not into that freaky stuff," she said firmly.

"Ok, baby," he said firmly.

She dressed in a white blouse and tight pink skirt manufactured from leather. She appeared good. She smelled sweet. We set there for a few hours enjoying a boxing match, drinking beer and smoking the coolest marijuana. Melvin never called. Mr. Lamont decided the nigga wasn't coming.

"Do you understand precisely why they call me the black widow?" she asked boldly, smiling.

"No, baby! I don't know," he said dryly.

"Because we love sex. Allow me to demonstrate honey," she said firmly.

Miss Gurry hopped on top of Mr. Lamont, unbuttoned his funky pants, and pulled them right down to his knees. She pulled down his crusty underwear full of doo-doo.

He smacked her across the face once or twice.

"You're a sizzling little lady. Let's find out how you black widows get down," Mr. Lamont stated cheerfully.

"When's the last time you changed your underwear?" she asked strongly, shaking her head greenly.

"Dude, a month ago, baby," he said sharply with a laugh.

She stared at his penis. She bit down on him and began eating.

Lamont began screaming. Blood ran down to the carpet.

"What did you do that for, lady?" Mr. Lamont said franticly.

"You desired to find out how we black widows make love. The female eats the males head off and he still does the thing. Then she finishes him off. And she eats a few of her babies. I'd three daughters and two sons. I ate both of my sons and one of my daughters," she explained sharply with a laugh.

"You crazy woman! Find me a doctor. Lord-Jesus somebody help me!" Mr. Lamont stated bluntly.

She had eaten most of him before heading over to the door. Lamont wasn't talking anymore. He was just a bloody mess. She had eaten half of him and there was from on the waist to his head left.

The dude's eyes were bulging, staring to the ceiling. He face was in shock.

"Next time be sure the woman's not really a black widow. And don't be so goddamn trustworthy. Besides, you're a major butt-breath." Then she walked out.

Melvin came in the door. Melvin took one look at his friend and saw all the blood he threw up and ran out of the place.

Where's Melvin?

A Mexican girl with cow eyes arrived, tall and sleek, wearing a strict pink dress. She smelled like honey. She strolled up to Mark Jones. He identified her as Claudia Hernandez, an ex-girlfriend. She'd a real creep brother Melvin Hernandez that hung around adolescent girls.

"What's up with ya, girl?" Jones said sharply with a smile, drinking a big bottle of Country Club beer.

"Have you seen, Melvin?" Claudia said strongly with a worried look.

"No, I haven't seen the bum. And I don't wish to," he stated harshly. "That bum owe me money!"

"You're intoxicated, Mark," she said sourly.

"I hope so, baby," he said strongly, taking a long sip.

"Did you choose to work to day?" she asked sharply.

"Hell no, girl," he snapped.

"Lazy!"

"Bruh, I got fired," he said sarcastically and took a long swig from the bottle.

"Sorry to hear that bro-bro," she said sadly.

"Let me tap that booty, girl! Bruh, it's been a while. You feel me?" he said strongly with a smile.

"Hell no, dog," she said hotly.

"Be cool, baby," he said strongly.

"How did you lose your job?" she asked firmly.

"Man, I was drunk and got into a fight," he said sharply.

"You're messed up, gee," she said sharply. "You know better than that!"

"Maybe!" he said strongly, finishing off the beer.

"Will you find Melvin?" She asked calmly.

"Hell no. I'm not a detective, dog! Besides, I'd rather eat pig turds. You feel me?" he said testily.

"I'll pay you. And you can have me if you'd like. You feel me?" she said sharply in a sad voice.

"Ok, fine. How much, blood?" Mr. Jones asked firmly.

"I'll give you $125.00," she said firmly.

"And that banging body of yours too, eh?" he said strongly with deep interest.

"Dog, if you like," she snapped.

"Oh, I like baby-girl!" he said cheerfully.

"And my mother and sister too," she said sharply.

"That's even better, baby," he said happily.

Mark Jones sat inside a bar known as Larry's Blue Bar. The bartender, Larry Zenos, was obviously a former NBA player. The pimp kept bring him Manhattan's and he drank them along with beer for a while. Zenos was awesome, but he wasn't stoned enough for Jones liking. A third-rate rapper, rapped about his awful life in Compton, CA. The bartender started weeping. The bum at the other end of the bar, smoking crack cocaine, pissed his pants, sobbed too. The lesbians smoked dope and cried too. Then the rapper began crying. The walls had graffiti, counter was gritty, tables were funky, floors were soaked with tears and chairs were awful to sit on. The place smelled like sweat, marijuana, crack cocaine and hog farts. Jones came here when he was depressed. A Mexican took his dishwasher employment because he got caught smoking marijuana while washing pots and pans. Before he left, he punched the Mexican in the face and hit the supervisor in the head with a big metal pot.

An Italian-looking girl sat down next to him. She looked incurably sad. She smelled like bug spray. She had blond freakish hair, big breast and booty. She was pulling on a joint.

"Hello, mister. My name is Huda Ciccone," she said cheerfully.

"Hiya. I'm Mark Jones. So what's up with ya? I used to be a dishwasher until some Mexican took my employment," he said strongly with a smirk.

"Don't hate on the Mexicans. My husband is Mexican. He's a good man," she said sharply.

"So why does the dude let you come in this dreadful joint?" Mr. Jones said strongly.

"He don't care," she snapped.

"Bruh, I think the homeboy's loco," he said sharply. "Baby, you're too fly. You feel me?"

"That's why we've been married so long. He does what he wants and I do the same."

"I was just smoking a little dope. But I did tell my boss to suck my banana's. You feel me?"

"You're just too lazy and a little stupid. It's tough to find a job in this economy, bruh," she said firmly.

"I know, mama," Mr. Jones said strongly.

The bartender delivered her a glass with some pink stuff. A sizable rat ran across the counter, big enough to ride. The rapper was singing an Ice Cube song. He sounded terrible. He slurred his words because he was incredibly drunk. A number of the words were completely wrong. This homeboy's band hip-hop beats were off key. He kept falling off the stage, but got back up. This bar was designed to perform blues, not rap. You feel me?

Mrs. Ciccone talked about her two felines arrested for stealing laptops and clothing from neighbor's backyards. And her daughter Fancy who kept setting herself on fire, because she idolized Joan of Arc. Her son Tom had runaway with a lizard woman to open a club selling marijuana. The authorities slain her pit-bull for attacking a little girl and raped her. Her husband paid teenage chicks working at McDonald's to have sex with him on top of their house.

"I'm going to kill myself," he said sharply, pouring beer all over the counter.

"I have a .45. Dude, you may borrow it," she said strongly with a smile. "I might need it back to use on myself too."

"Sure, I'll have my ghost take it back to you. You feel me?" he said.

"Great."

Jones drank his ninth Manhattan. Some nasty people wearing tattoos came in with their sick-looking dogs, smoking marijuana. They sat down at a table, crying.

A man with lizard skin smoking a massive joint threw a shot-glass at the rapper. "My grandmother raps better than that guy," he shouted sharply.

The homeboy got angry and hopped from the stage, brought out a nine inch blade, rammed it into the lizard man's chest, pulled it out, shoved it back in. The lizard man screamed like a girl. They smashed some chairs and tables on each other.

While the lizard man was on the floor, the rapper kicked that bum in the head. When he got up, he staggered over to the bar. Larry passed him a bottle of Cobra light beer. The rapper went back to the stage as if nothing occurred. The lizard man got up holding his chest, green blood leaked out. He walked out of the tavern and nobody ever seen him again.

Mark Jones appeared to be a black man that washed vehicles. He had no education-maybe on the street. He wandered into Al's Arcade, where Melvin hung out. It had become a scandalous place. This dude sold Marijuana and cocaine to the teenagers that came in here to play pinball. He got teen girls stoned and so they had sex in the bathroom with him. Most detrimental things could happen to North Berkeley. He observed chatting and joshing. The pinball and video game sounds gave Mr. Jones a headache.

Al, a cynical bag of guts walked over to him. He was brawny, and bald. He wore a low priced blue shirt and blue jeans. He smelled like sewage.

"Hey, I don't allow any slimy alkies in here," he said bluntly.

"In that case you shouldn't be here either. You feel me?" Jones said firmly.

"What do you want maggot?" Al asked brazenly.

"Looking for Melvin," Mr. Jones said firmly.

"As you can observe the poop-eater ain't here. Dude, I can't stand the butt worm. He constantly comes in here smoking that stuff. And touching the high school females in unacceptable areas. He sells dope to the teenage boys," Al explained harshly.

"Yeh, a real winner," Jones said strongly with a smirk.

"Get lost doo-doo breath," Al said sourly.

"Where did he go, dog?" Jones asked bluntly.

"Don't know, frog-poop! Don't care," Al snapped.

"Do you ever wipe your booty?" Jones asked sharply.

"Slime you, bruh," Al said irately.

"Dude, make sure the next time you wipe that all the brown stuff is all gone," Mr. Jones suggested firmly.

Al didn't answer, his face hardened.

Jones pressed his finger up against Al's throat. The man started to choke. Consequently, he gave in.

"Okay, homeboy. Mary Heimdall, a blond bum, with a face like an ape. I swear dog. A monster wouldn't go down on that lady. She lives in a rat-hole on West 7th Street," Al explained strongly.

"Thanks, pig-poop," Mr. Jones said sharply, strolled into the restroom, and pooped on the floor.

Jones sat in Miss Heimdall's terrible apartment in West Oakland. She was sucking on a crack-pipe. He couldn't imagine any individual was that hideous. A dude she referred to as Mike appeared to be a bum, set on the sofa naked, drinking a huge bottle Budweiser and smoking marijuana.

"So you haven't seen Melvin, brother?" Jones asked strongly.

"Two nights ago, he came over. Dude, we got high and had outrageous sex and neighbors called the po-pos," she boasted sharply with a smile.

"Cool," Jones said firmly.

"It was, baby," she said cheerfully.

"You know where I could find him?" Jones asked seriously.

"Are you the po-pos?" she asked strongly.

"Hell no, girl! If I was I'd run your pungent butt in for smoking that stuff. You feel me?" Mr. Jones said bluntly.

"Dude, he's possibly with that Spanish broad," Mike added sharply.

Jones visited Imbach's Smoke Shop& Grill--- cheesy place. That bum Imbach always had young strippers on stage; having untamed sex with everybody who arrived, however, many looked twelve or younger. Many weird folks came in there, trashing the spot. The law came often. They didn't sell beer. They only sold marijuana, cocaine, Atropine, Bête-nut, Codeine and Crack—you name it. Folks came in to try to do drugs, eat and catch smutty sex entertainment. If you didn't use drugs you couldn't come inside. On one occasion, he saw a police officer in there, having sex with a blond about fifteen and they got high together. You needed to be high to relish the shows. On Thursday nights, Imbach might have some pretty young man go on stage and do some porn stuff with the girls. On Friday nights, the hottest and youngest black females would take the stage, strip, sing and get high and have wild sex with everybody on the stage. Gay night was on Monday. He heard a lot of outrageous gay sex went on. There were all types came in. They played hip-hop music and rock. Mr. Jones smoked three joints. He ate a couple of hot-dogs and fries. The hotdogs tasted spoiled. While sitting at the bar a Chinese girl was kissing him. When he didn't find Melvin here, he left. He threw up those hot-dogs on the street.

When Jones pasted Pluto's Night Club his luck changed. Melvin, the little brown runt came out of the spot with a raggedy blond. She was lanky, wearing a tight pink dress crafted from cotton and much needed a bath. These folks were both smoking marijuana and sharing a big bottle of Cobra. She didn't have much sense if she was with that dude.

"Hey, Melvin," Jones said strongly with a smirk.

"Hey, yourself, Jones. What is it? You can't locate any bars?" Melvin said sharply with a laugh.

"Lose the broad! Homeboy, we've got to chat," Mr. Jones said firmly.

"Broad. Screw you, mister," she snapped.

"Anytime sleaze," Mr. Jones said strongly with a grin.

"Yeah. Bug off, bruh," Melvin said hotly.

"Blood, it's important. Bruh, it's Claudia," Mr. Jones said seriously.

"Are you gonna let this piece of dog-poop call me a sleaze and get away with it?" she screamed.

"Go on, boo. I'll catch up with you later. You feel me?" Melvin said strongly.

She went away mad.

"Why didn't she come herself?" Melvin asked hotly.

"I don't know, dog," Mr. Jones snapped.

"I'm not going back to that lousy farm, bruh," Melvin said defensively.

"I don't care, gee," Mr. Jones said hotly.

"Claudia just needs me to clean up horse doo-doo. Bruh, it might take me a year. Dog, I'm not down with that. You hear what I'm saying?" Melvin said hotly.

"That's your issue frog-breath. Now come on," Mr. Jones said harshly, grabbing his arm and squeezing tight.

Melvin yanked it back. He then smacked Jones in the face, hard enough to knock him on the ground. Jones got back up but as he did Melvin kicked him in the shin with steel-toe boots and Jones bent over and grabbed his shin, wincing in pain. Melvin kicked him in the chest and Jones fell backwards onto his back. Then Melvin pissed on him. Then he ran off across the street like a little coward.

When Jones got up, he threw up orange blue stuff on his shoes. Melvin was long gone. Just for this to make love with Claudia. He should be able to make love to her entire family for life and a condominium in the hills.

By noon, Jones quit. The dude wandered the neighborhood trying to find bars. He chucked stones at a number of shop windows. As soon as he pasted by the Greyhound Bus station he stumbled upon Melvin. He seemed to be hauling a funky dark tote in the direction of the restroom. Jones went in there after him.

Jones was standing by the doorway of the restroom, holding his right shoe. Once Melvin arrived on the scene rapping Mo Money Mo Problems by The Notorious B.I.G. Featuring P. Diddy& Mase, he struck him dead center in the face with all the heel of his shoe---hard. His nose made a crunch sound. Melvin let out a loud scream like a girl, releasing the tote bag and grabbing hold of his nose. But Jones kept bashing him in the face, drawing lots of blood until the heel broke-off. Blood ran out of his nose and mouth.

"You bum! Dog, you broke my bleeping nose," he cried.

"You pissed on me punk. Dog, I consider us even. Let's visit your sister bruh," Jones snapped.

"How did you locate me, dog?" Melvin asked sharply.

"I'm a detective, bruh!" Mr. Jones said hotly.

"You ain't any detective! You're a slimy dishwasher," Melvin said harshly.

Jones had taken Melvin's butt outside the bus station without any hassle.

"Where were you headed, dog?" Mr. Jones asked.

"Honduras."

"Nice getaway."

"Get me a physician, homeboy," Melvin cried sharply.

When Melvin and Mr. Jones arrived at Claudia's farm, he locked one of his ankles to a shackle while naked.

"Very good," she said cheerfully.

"Bruh, I thought you'd enjoy it. This dude can't leave until he is done cleaning up all the horse poop," Mr. Jones said sharply with a grin.

"Remove this shackle, frog-poop! I'm no slave, homeboy. You hear what I'm saying?" Melvin said gruffly.

"Watch your mouth, bro-bro," she said hotly.

"I'm not an animal, dog," Melvin said hotly.

"I know. You're most horrible as compared to an animal, bruh," Jones stated strongly, kicking him.

"Screw you. You alky-bum! Look what he did to my nose, sis?" Melvin said bitterly.

"The jerk pissed on me," Mr. Jones said maliciously.

"You shouldn't have come on like a punk," Melvin snapped.

"Dude, I say it's a vast improvement," she said cheerfully.

"I'll sue the two of you," Melvin said firmly.

"Stop being a little girl, bro-bro," Mr. Jones snapped. "It's not like you're eating pig poop!"

"Slime you, bum!" Melvin said firmly.

"When he cleans up all the poop, this key will unlock the shackles. You feel me?" Mr. Jones said strongly with a smirk.

"I got you," she said firmly.

"I need some bleeping clothes. Dude, it's chilly throughout the night. Bruh, you can't leave me outdoors. You hear what I'm saying?" Melvin cried.

"Quiet, homeboy!" Mr. Jones said bluntly.

"Now I would like to consume your body," Jones said strongly with a smile as big as a home. "Let's visit your bedroom, dog."

"No, right here, dog," she ordered firmly.

"Okay, whatever," Mr. Jones said cheerfully.

Her mother entered the barn and her sister too.

The lady moved those fragile hands inside the flowery dress and yanked down her panties, halting at the knobby knees. Her mother and sister did the same task.

Jones was attacked by her brother and raped who was wearing a dress. Claudia and her mother ran out of there.

"Help me!" Mr. Jones said savagely.

"How do you like it bum?" her brother said firmly.

"Help me!" Jones cried.

After the bother finished he kicked Jones in the stomach a couple of times and he threw up. And the brother tossed two hundred dollar bills on him and walked off.

Jones quickly grabbed the money and slowly and he went along to the closest tavern.

Incident At Watts Meat Market

"You slut!" Mr. Watts stated hotly.

"You ignorant-fool!" Mrs. Watts said acidly.

"Home-girl, you cheated on me!" he stated defensively.

"You cheated on me dog. Dude, you should put a lock on your private parts," she said harshly.

"Can you prove it, girl?" he snapped.

"Hell, yes, poop-breath," she said emotionally.

"Bruh, you got pictures girl?" he said strongly.

"Miesha, she took photos of your butt leaving this girl's apartment in North Reno," she said strongly, shoving the pictures in his face.

He studied them for a moment and shook his head.

"Homegirl, this ain't me. This cat looks too fat and ugly and stupid," he said hotly. Besides Miesha is a bleeping crack cocaine whore and don't know nothing!"

"It is too," she snapped. "I believe her bruh."

He threw the pictures on the floor.

"You made love to our neighbor," he said vociferously.

"Maybe if you treat a sister-girl better she wouldn't go elsewhere," she said firmly.

After that, this Chinese dude entered on crutches and struggled up to the cash register. The spot was in fact cleaned out. No people. He then brought up a Beretta .32 with a silencer in their face, showing no fear of these black folks.

"Yo, open the register, broad!" Mr. Wong instructed harshly with deep Chinese accent.

"You don't speak to my wife that way, dude," Mr. Watts proclaimed gruffly.

"That's correct, punk," Mrs. Watts pointed out.

"Homegirl, I can't believe we're being robbed by an oriental," Larry stated strongly in disbelief.

"Shut up, people! Give me the money!" Wong said bluntly.

"A homeboy can't have nothing without someone trying to clown us," she said hotly.

"This cat told me to shut up. You messing-up now," Mr. Watts said caustically. "I might have to check you fool!"

The man shoved the gun barrel in the woman's left breast. "Dude, I'll blow this woman's breast away," Wong said bitterly.

"Okay, baby! We better do what that slimy-nut says," she explained strongly.

"Easy. Come on, baby-boy. Dude, we'll get your cash," Mr. Watts stated nervously. "Why you robbing poor black folks?"

Mrs. Watts opened up the draw and nervously picked up the bills and coins, losing a few on the floor.

"Hurry up, sister. Dude, I ain't got all day," the man stated strongly.

She emerged about the countertop and with all the cash.

"Here, sir," she said calmly.

"Put it on the table, homegirl!" Wong said sharply.

She placed all of it on the table.

Wong grunted as he battled his way over to the table, with the firearm still on them.

"I know very well what you are planning. And you better in no way try it either. Homeboy, I may be a handicap, however, I'm no hoodwink using a pistol," Wong explained snugly.

Wong sat down on one of the plastic-type seats.

His full name was in fact James Wong, and financial advisor. He appeared to be in horrible condition. He appeared as if a lion chewed on him and spit him out. His head of hair seemed to be kinky. He'd horrendous zits, wore thick lens spectacles, left side of his face had been eliminated, his brownish suit seemed to be wrinkled. He smelled just as if he didn't wipe his booty decent. He was in fact sardonic. He was belligerent, extreme and astute. He sat there counting the funds, as the Watts stood there bewildered.

"Dog, this is it, $100.00?" Wong said hotly.

"That's it, dog. Now jet, baby," Mr. Watts said firmly. "We're poor black people baby!"

"This joint doesn't possess a safe?" Wong asked sharply.

"Naw, bruh," Mr. Watts snapped.

"Somehow I don't believe you bum," Wong said suspiciously.

"Well, it's correct, gangsta," Mrs. Watts said strongly.

"You have a billfold, Homeboy?" Wong asked sharply.

"Hell, yes, bruh," Mr. Watts stated strongly.

"Girl, you have a handbag?" Wong asked firmly.

"Of course, dog," she stated calmly.

"Everything on the table, lady," Wong explained crudely, gawking incredulously.

Mrs. Watts dumped her buckskin handbag on top of the table, scattering every little thing about. Certainly, there had been lipstick, tampons, mascara, tobacco, change, postage stamps, fingernail polish kit, hair brushes, change-purse, contraception, a couple of joints, mace and a comb, a cellphone, car keys. Mr. Watts had taken out three hundred dollar bills and positioned them on the table. Furthermore, a couple of condoms dropped from his wallet. There were two quarters and two pep capsules (amphetamines) in his pockets.

Wong nabbed up the change-purse. He opened up it and poured every little thing out. There had been three twenty dollar bills, six one-dollar bills and dimes, quarters, pennies plus some nickels. He placed virtually all of it in his pockets. He smashed the cell phones. Likewise, he had taken one of the joints.

"Birth control, lady?" Mr. Watts said savagely.

"Bruh, I don't need to have anymore crack babies, homey," she said bitterly.

"It's that neighbor you been seeing," Mr. Watts said frigidly.

"So what, dog?" she shouted sharply.

"I'm going to smoke that cat like a cigar," Mr. Watts said firmly.

"I'm going to smoke your but gee, if you touch him," she said maliciously, punching him in the face.

Mr. Watts didn't hit her back.

"Where is that frog-breath now?" Larry said sharply, walking away as she kept slugging him. "Your butt don't have nothing to say now do ya?"

"Knock that stuff off," Wong said sharply with eyes seething.

"Rubbers for that woman, eh?" she snapped.

"My plan wasn't to get this broad pregnant," Larry said strongly.

"How come her butt ain't here dog?" she snapped.

"I didn't call her!" he said strongly.

"Bleep you, homeboy! I despise your cheating butt," she mentioned hotly. "What's that slimy woman's name?"

"None of your business baby!" Larry snapped.

Mrs. Watts began punching and kicking Larry again. The brother still wouldn't attack back. He just kept walking away.

"I would like a divorce!" she said sharply.

"You got it, dog," he stated strongly.

"Shut the hell up! Wong proclaimed hotly. "Calm down. Homey, I really mean it, or I'll waste both of you."

"How do you believe you are able to rob us as well as get away with it on crutches? No dude would likely be that ignorant," Mr. Watts said strongly.

"Are you calling me ignorant, punk?" Wong questioned strongly, waving the pistol.

"You ought to check him, bruh," she stated sardonically.

"No, you ought to get rid of her and save me the hassle," Mr. Watts said bluntly.

"No, eliminate him simply because I'm the much better cook," she said strongly. "And you can make love to me!"

"A pathetic $926.89," Wong stated brazenly with eyes raking the room.

"Why? We have no beef with our Asian brothers," Mr. Watts claimed sharply.

"I don't hate on the brothers. I didn't know you were black folks," Wong stated strongly, placing the cash in his pocket. "Dude, I actually just came in here to hide."

"Now, you realize, baby, that gangster's are up in this joint," Mr. Watts explained strongly with a predatory expression.

"I'm still retaining the cash, dog," Wong mentioned snugly. "You don't scare me homeboy!"

There had been a lengthy glass counter. Right at the end, the glass was smashed, as if somebody had punched it. It had been stuffed with delicious meats such as turkey, ground beef, pork, horsemeat, goat-meat, dog-meat, catfish, shrimp, cat-meat, raccoon-meat, human-leg, camel-meat, human-meat, duck-meat, crow, rib's, alligator-meat, rattlesnake, Natural and organic snake eggs, pig-feet, sheep-meat, quid, bear-meat, salmon, crab, Sweet Zombie brains, human-meat, salami, sausage, corn-beef, roast-beef, lamb, frog-legs, chitterlings, duck, beef tongue, donkey penis, monkey-brains, liver, beef and pork penis and balls, human-heart, kidneys, pork-bowels, chicken, milk and eggs.

There seemed to be a small snack-bar. Plus some lousy plastic-type kitchen tables with chairs. There was in fact a busted pinball machine in the corner. A number of the tables had tic-tac-toe scribbled on them. One particular had Sarah Butler provides fantastic weed call 775-345-2389. To make love with an actual vampire call 775-675-6129. And the other stated Blowjob Anderson dined right here and threw up. I had made love to my Mom on this table and got STD. My wife sucks every dude's cock that comes in here. I want to eat good pussy who do I call. Peter and Tony had a sperm guzzling contest while eating here. If you're a parent and would really like your kids to be molested or have group sex call Al at 775-329-6347. If you want a job that pays $45 dollars an hour dressing up like a chicken and running through traffic all day, please call Tom at 775-322-6953 while positions are still open. If you would like to date women from Mars please call Tina at 775-821-1129. Wong had taken out a jar with white powder in it. He poured the stuff out onto a handkerchief. Utilizing a part of a matchbook, he shaped the white powder into lengthy lines. He rolled $ 1 bill and placed it up his left nostril. Pressing a finger on the other nostril, he bent over one of the white lines and sniffed. Then repeated the same thing with the other lines.

Furthermore, Watts marketed marijuana and crack cocaine. He at the same time placed the drugs in the meats. His spot kept chaotic everyday. The foolish cops never assumed anything. Even a few of his customers were cops.

"Homeboy? Why are you so messed up?" Mr. Watts questioned strongly with a smirk.

"That brat. My lady had been a stunning girl. Her name was Ruth. At some point, I had been high on cocaine when I noticed her flirting with a lesbian in the Safeway. Once we got outside, we strolled up to the car and I started out beating my blond lady. Dude, I did her real ugly; her face would be a bloody mess. Next, all these nosy punks dived in and nabbed me. The Reno cops had taken me to jail. Because if they didn't I would've beaten that woman so bad her mother wouldn't have recognized her. She wouldn't press charges therefore they released me. After that one day I'd been waiting in the driveway, Ruth pulled up and ran my ass down. While I was underneath the car, she backed up and driven down the street---fast. She dragged my butt several miles down the avenue. After a little luck I rolled from underneath the car," Wong explained sharply.

"Lord, what a tale. She certainly messed you up," Mrs. Watts added sharply with a laugh.

"Enough talk. I'm famished. What's decent?" Wong asked strongly.

"Bro-bro, I suggest the dog-meat," she proclaimed confidently.

"Dude, I'll check it out. I never ate dog before. Dude, I'd like tomatoes, lettuce, don't forget the onions, cheese, plenty of mustard and mayo, with pickles-on whole wheat bread," Wong instructed sharply.

"Then, you desire everything?" She said calmly.

"That's correct, girl," Wong snapped.

Mrs. Watts wiggled her small high butt up to the kitchen counter and wandered around to begin her task of making him a sandwich.

"What booty?" Wong shouted sharply with a grin.

"Look at your own lady," Mr. Watts stated strongly.

"Look at me, brother. No woman wishes to hook up with my butt," Wong stated regretfully. "I'm all messed up, gee."

"Don't lose faith, dude. There are plenty of frantic broads to choose from," Mr. Watts explained strongly with a laugh.

"Because of that lady I've experienced several skin operations. That's the reason I don't have a booty no more. My daughter is really a skeleton for donating a great deal of skin. I've headaches on a regular basis. Dude I doo-doo diarrhea through a tube. It looks just like blue soup. My left leg had been assembled with bird wire. Youngsters stare as well as make jokes," Wong explained sharply.

"Don't worry, bruh. I know a lot of women that will kick-it with you," Mr. Watts said strongly.

Larry Watts appeared to be a lemon-yellow black man, tall and virile. He seemed to be in a fit condition. He turned out to be deficient on the insightfulness department. He'd a pacifistic manner.

Cecil Watts appeared to be Vanessa Williams. She came across as perceptive, friendly and quirky. She delivered a massive sandwich on a small plate and sat it in the front of Wong. As soon as she wandered away, he smacked her on the rear end with his crutch. She gave a stony expression.

Wong dug in the sandwich just like a manic. Mr. Watts delivered him a bottle of Country Club beer to wash down the sandwich. When he polished off the meal, he chucked the dish on the wall and it smashed into pieces.

"That's decent china," Mrs. Watts complained bluntly.

"Not anymore," Wong stated sharply with a laugh.

"When are you planning to depart?" Mrs. Watts requested irately.

"When I feel like it, people," Wong snapped.

"You've all of our cash, bruh. Why stay?" Mr. Watts said firmly.

"The cops happen to be after me. Brother---Just like, I stated previously. I require a spot to hide. I discovered my wife having sex with a woman therefore; I shot both of them using this firearm. Consequently don't push me brother, murdering is less difficult the third time. So you'd better do every little thing I say to you, dog," Wong explained snugly.

"You're a slime ball, dog," Mr. Watts mentioned harshly.

"Maybe. This had taken a while, bruh. I'd been shoved over the perimeter. My job---I had been the only Chinese there. Dude, I became under a great deal of damn stress. I'm fed up with people making a hoodwink out of me," Mr. Wong said moodily.

"What do you do for a living?" Mr. Watts asked strongly.

"An Accountant for major electronics firm until my lady messed me up," Wong said harshly.

"Sounds fly," she said firmly.

"Yeah, and you?" Wong asked calmly.

"Child, you see it. This dude and I sell meat all day---everyday," she answered sharply with a bored look.

"Well, the simple truth is, I can't stay. Dude, I got a conference with the Wolf Pack team," Mr. Watts said calmly.

"So you play basketball? I should have guessed. Okay proceed for your meeting. Don't attempt anything. In the event you retrieve the cops, this bimbo gets it, and as much people I could find long before the cops get hold of me, okay? Do I make myself crystal-clear?" Wong said strongly.

"Sure, old blood," Mr. Watts proclaimed strongly.

"Mr. Wong, I will help you escape I've a car," she insisted sharply. "The cops wouldn't anticipate you having a gorgeous sister," Mrs. Watts explained sharply with a smirk.

"Sounds awesome. However, you realize I'll need to get rid of Mr. Watts," Wong mentioned regretfully.

"Well, that's okay. Bruh, I had been intending to divorce the homeboy anyway," she said sharply.

"Slime you, dog! Bruh, I adore you, girl," Mr. Watts said hotly. "And this is how you do me?"

"Besides this dreadful bleeping meat business is actually a bore, bro-bro," she stated harshly, frowning.

"I discovered your sorry butt grooving inside a pathetic third-rate topless tavern. Bruh, I had taken you away from all that bull," Mr. Watts stated firmly.

"Shut up. You're both giving me a bleeping headache! My dog, I stated close it. Or perhaps I'll utilize this weapon to get it done. You're not heading anyplace and neither will you be, baby," Wong stated gruffly. "Brother, I have to ponder. Therefore, shut up. Allow me to think."

There seemed to be a yellowish man in a picture on the wall. He'd a white Afro, positioned there with James Brown, Muddy Waters and Marvin Gaye. Wong stared at the images for a time.

"I didn't have any idea James Brown ate in this rat-hole," James said strongly with a laugh.

"Yes, Mr. Wong. That's correct. That's my dad. He's retired these days. He played the drums with Muddy Waters. Real awesome, huh?" Mr. Watts said strongly with a smile, holding his crotch.

"Yeah, cool," Wong responded dryly.

Things had been calm for some time Wong sat there snorting cocaine and drinking Country Club beer. At some point, it appeared as if the ignorant-fool smeared his face with flour. Mrs. Watts lit up a major joint and switched on the radio to some rap station. Next, she swayed her hips to hip-hop beats, taking in extended pulls from her joint and sang out the lyrics horribly. Wong pissed on the floor due to the fact he couldn't reach the toilet.

"Are you insane, dog?" Mr. Watts said sharply.

"Mr. Watts, you shouldn't have offered me all of this beer. As a result I couldn't hold it," he stated calmly.

Mrs. Watts provided Mr. Watts a hit from the joint.

"Come here, baby," Wong inquired sharply.

"Why, Mr. Wong?" she said strongly.

"Because I'm keen on you, baby. Besides I'm in the mood for chocolate cake," Wong said boldly with a laugh.

"And if I don't?" she shot back.

"Then I'll blast ya, boo," Mr. Wong said firmly.

Mrs. Watts came over.

"Kiss me girl. Conduct it now," Wong instructed strongly.

"Hell no, nigga," Mr. Watts yelled strongly. "You ain't kissing my woman."

"Back off, bruh!" Mr. Wong proclaimed harshly to Mr. Watts. "You're likely to be a part of the fun as well. You're going to kiss me, bruh. Dude; I never kissed a pretty dude like you before."

"Like hell. I'm not gay. Slime you dog," Mr. Watts proclaimed candidly.

"Dog...I'll shoot you and also her. Dog, you don't want to piss me off," Wong explained sharply.

Mrs. Watts made out with Wong for a while. After they finished making love she made love to her husband. Then all three made love.

The gangster rap tunes played on loudly. Folks tapped on the window, but no-one opened up the door. They continued to have wild sex.

The cops came by searching for Mr. Wong, yet Mr. Watts told them practically nothing. That homeboy dealt with it wisely; due to the fact, Wong had the pistol directed at the back of his head.

"What's in this room, dog?" Wong requested strongly, aiming his crutch at the door.

"Nothing...just an office, dog," Mrs. Watts explained sharply.

"Bull, home-girl! Dude, is there a safe inside?" Mr. Wong asked strongly.

"I don't know, man," Mr. Watts clarified strongly.

"Unlock that thing and less find out, bruh. Every joint includes a safe," Mr. Wong proclaimed sharply, striving to move in the direction of the door.

"We very much ghetto in this joint," Mr. Watts said firmly with a smile.

"Homeboy, open the door!" Wong ordered moodily. "Before I check you gee!"

Mr. Watts unlocked the door. A scraped up desk had taken up half of the office space, filing cabinets and also a compact wall safe in the back. There were a bunch of empty Coke, Cobra and Olde English cans on the floor.

"Open the safe, baby!" Wong instructed venomously.

"Dog, I forgot the damn combination," Mr. Watts snapped.

Wong placed the gun barrel against Mr. Watts's head. "Brother, open up the bleeping safe!"

Mr. Watts opened up the safe. He had taken out a bag of marijuana and $45,000 in cash.

"Wow. Exactly where did all this come from, player?" Larry stated strongly with a laugh to Wong.

Wong mashed the base of the crutch against Mr. Watts's skull. "I ought to take you out, brother. Homeboy, I'm not a man you want to mess with," Wong said indignantly.

Mr. Watts rubbed his head.

"That hurts, player," Mr. Watts stated bluntly.

"Hurry up. Place this stuff inside the tote," Wong directed hotly.

"Child, I'll help," Mrs. Watts insisted calmly.

"Tonight, I'm leaving with your lady dog," Wong proclaimed boldly with a smirk.

"What about me, gee?" Mr. Watts questioned sharply.

"I'm likely to slaughter you, bro-bro," Wong explained hotly.

"No, please, sir. Don't kill my hubby," she cried.

"Shut up, homegirl! Grab the tote," Wong stated strongly.

"Now what, pimp?" Mr. Watts inquired strongly.

"Once I'm safe I'll plant this slut," Wong said sharply.

"No, you won't, poop-breath," she proclaimed harshly.

Wong positioned the weapon to her head.

"I'll slay you here, dog," Wong mentioned snugly.

"Larry...baby...please," she pleaded loudly.

"Not so harsh now, homegirl," Wong said calmly with a smile.

"Don't worry. I'll save you, boo," Mr. Watts proclaimed sharply.

Mr. Watts came up for Wong and he elevated the firearm. Next Mrs. Watts swung the tote, striking the cripple man around the shoulder. The firearm went off. Mr. Watts grabbed hold of Wong striking him in the face---he released the gun and crutches as he fell backwards. Definitely, now the man appeared to be out cold.

"Baby, are you all right?" Mr. Watts said sharply.

"Yes, my boo-boo," Mrs. Watts said clearly.

"I'm bleeding. This damn fool got me in the left ear," he stated sadly.

"Is it bad?" she said sharply.

"Naw, I'll live," he said strongly with a grin.

"What now, baby?" she asked nervously.

"Let's phone the po-pos," he advised strongly. "So they can get this sorry bleeding bum off our floor."

"Blood, we'll be town heroes for bring in a killer," she proclaimed strongly with a big smile.

"It's all gravy baby. Nonetheless, what about us?" he said strongly.

"I'm not divorcing you, dog. Baby, you saved my life. Bruh, I've got nothing but love for you, dog," she explained sharply with a smile.

"I adore you more than ever before, boo. Will you marry me again, babygirl?" he said strongly with a smile.

"Yes, child," she said cheerfully, jumping on him and kissing him.

THE END

About The Author

I live somewhere in Berkeley and have lived in Nevada. I worked as a busboy while writing stuff about Russia. From there I studied writing at a community collage but because of alcohol problems, I missed a lot of classes. I wrote a potent small collection of stories called The Crimes In File No. 9. My goal is to get a million readers because reading is very important and so many people can't read. I want to end this especially in poor neighborhoods. If you have a copy of this book, I want to thank you for your support.